Which Season and
What Colors
are the Essence of You?

MARTHA

I dedicate this book with profound gratitude to my genius and loving mentor, Anahita Joon Tehrani, for elegantly escorting me into my Divine Feminine Embodiment Transformation.

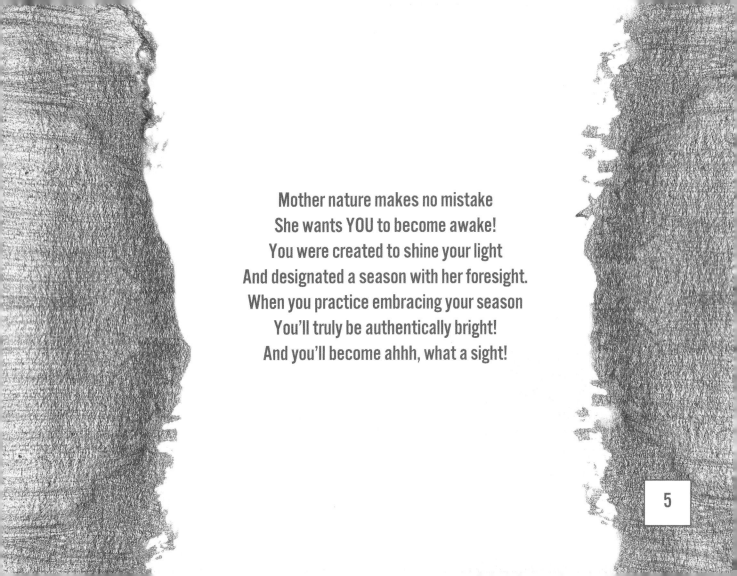

Mother nature makes no mistake
She wants YOU to become awake!
You were created to shine your light
And designated a season with her foresight.
When you practice embracing your season
You'll truly be authentically bright!
And you'll become ahhh, what a sight!

People around you will gasp, as you align with her deliberate intention.
You see, when your season is actualized within you, you become the manifestation of divine invention!
The environments of your inner and outer being harmonize,
affecting your ability to socialize
both with yourself and the people you see.
Relaxation and connection happen, inspired by your glorious embodiment to be.
Most importantly however, you get to dwell more comfortably in thee!

8

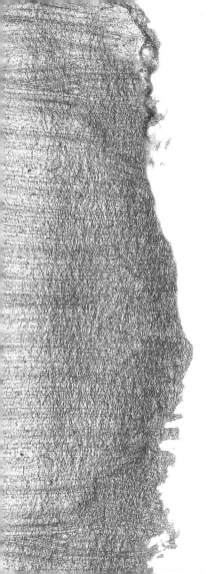

So, which season is the essence of you?

Now, my love, please take heed,
Your preferences have no place here—
they actually make you blunder,
And I want you to feel wonder.
Judgments and woundings prevent you
from embodying the essence of you.
So here, let's be careful what you do:
Each season is equally magical
So please be open to your season as potentially
fantastical?
The earth has four seasons offering us diversity
So when you learn your season, I encourage you to
breathe through a knee jerk adversity.

So, which season is the essence of you?

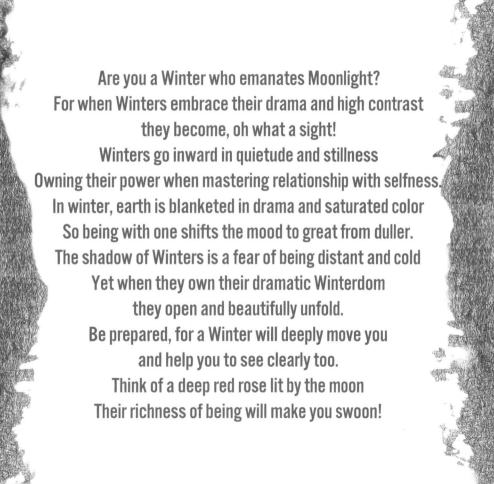

Are you a Winter who emanates Moonlight?
For when Winters embrace their drama and high contrast
they become, oh what a sight!
Winters go inward in quietude and stillness
Owning their power when mastering relationship with selfness.
In winter, earth is blanketed in drama and saturated color
So being with one shifts the mood to great from duller.
The shadow of Winters is a fear of being distant and cold
Yet when they own their dramatic Winterdom
they open and beautifully unfold.
Be prepared, for a Winter will deeply move you
and help you to see clearly too.
Think of a deep red rose lit by the moon
Their richness of being will make you swoon!

11

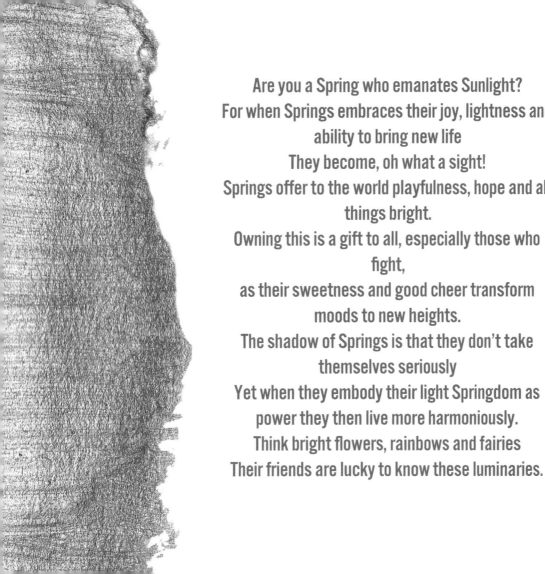

Are you a Spring who emanates Sunlight?
For when Springs embraces their joy, lightness and
ability to bring new life
They become, oh what a sight!
Springs offer to the world playfulness, hope and all
things bright.
Owning this is a gift to all, especially those who
fight,
as their sweetness and good cheer transform
moods to new heights.
The shadow of Springs is that they don't take
themselves seriously
Yet when they embody their light Springdom as
power they then live more harmoniously.
Think bright flowers, rainbows and fairies
Their friends are lucky to know these luminaries.

14

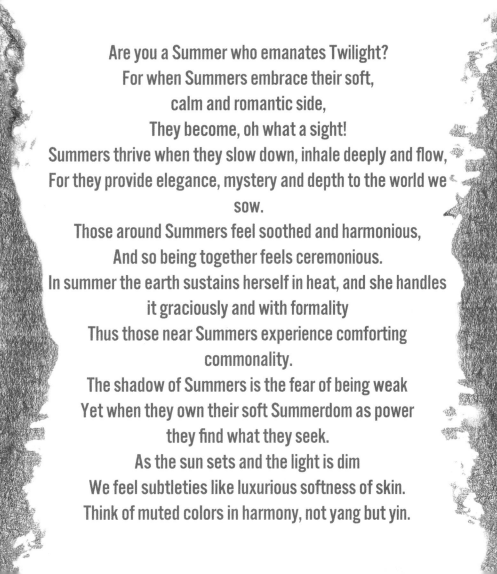

Are you a Summer who emanates Twilight?
For when Summers embrace their soft,
calm and romantic side,
They become, oh what a sight!
Summers thrive when they slow down, inhale deeply and flow,
For they provide elegance, mystery and depth to the world we
sow.
Those around Summers feel soothed and harmonious,
And so being together feels ceremonious.
In summer the earth sustains herself in heat, and she handles
it graciously and with formality
Thus those near Summers experience comforting
commonality.
The shadow of Summers is the fear of being weak
Yet when they own their soft Summerdom as power
they find what they seek.
As the sun sets and the light is dim
We feel subtleties like luxurious softness of skin.
Think of muted colors in harmony, not yang but yin.

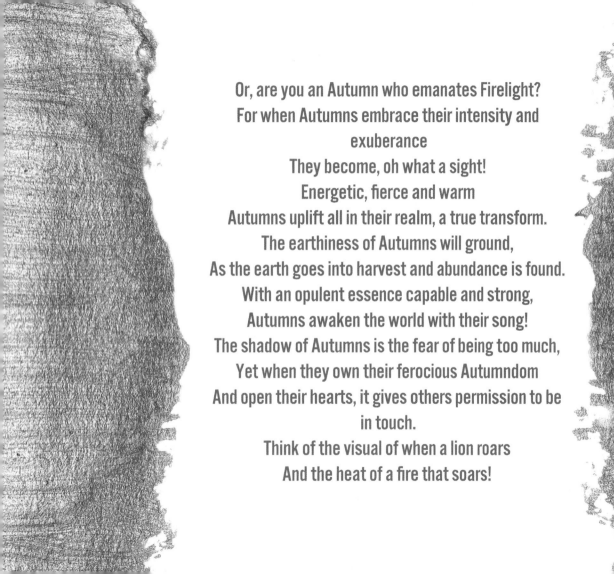

Or, are you an Autumn who emanates Firelight?
For when Autumns embrace their intensity and exuberance
They become, oh what a sight!
Energetic, fierce and warm
Autumns uplift all in their realm, a true transform.
The earthiness of Autumns will ground,
As the earth goes into harvest and abundance is found.
With an opulent essence capable and strong,
Autumns awaken the world with their song!
The shadow of Autumns is the fear of being too much,
Yet when they own their ferocious Autumndom
And open their hearts, it gives others permission to be in touch.
Think of the visual of when a lion roars
And the heat of a fire that soars!

17

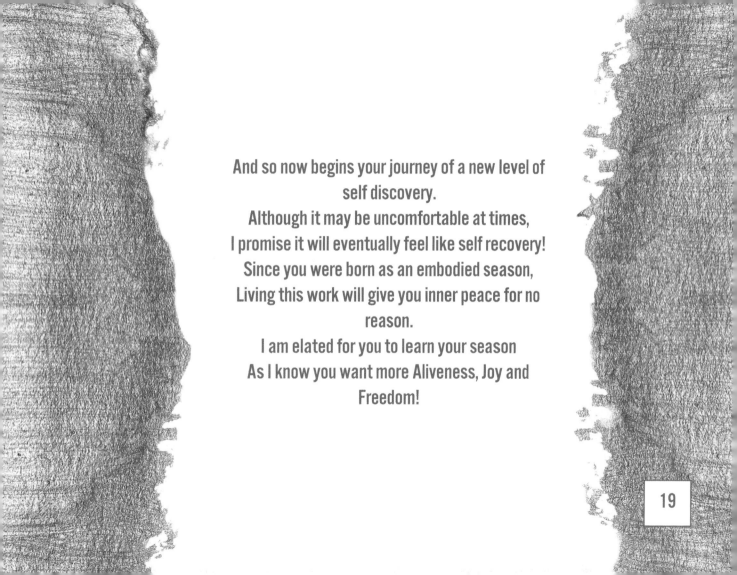

And so now begins your journey of a new level of self discovery.
Although it may be uncomfortable at times,
I promise it will eventually feel like self recovery!
Since you were born as an embodied season,
Living this work will give you inner peace for no reason.
I am elated for you to learn your season
As I know you want more Aliveness, Joy and Freedom!

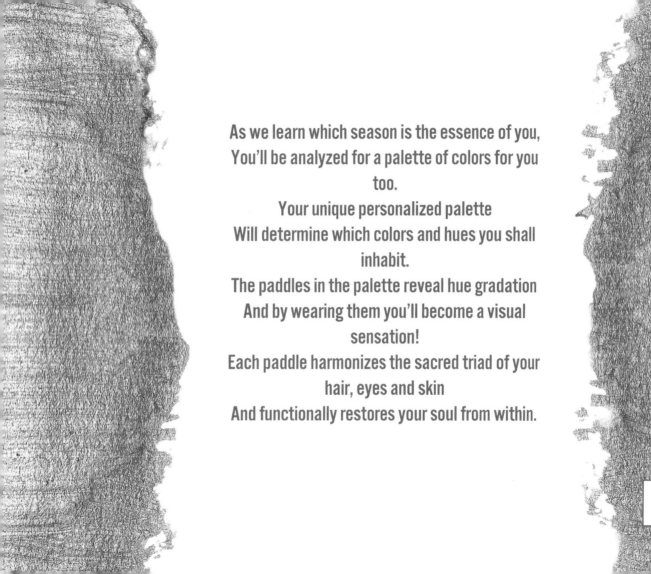

As we learn which season is the essence of you,
You'll be analyzed for a palette of colors for you too.
Your unique personalized palette
Will determine which colors and hues you shall inhabit.
The paddles in the palette reveal hue gradation
And by wearing them you'll become a visual sensation!
Each paddle harmonizes the sacred triad of your hair, eyes and skin
And functionally restores your soul from within.

Mother Nature created you as a work of art
And so understanding your color signature will
open your heart, both to yourself and the people
you know,
Opening your life to an abundance of flow.
Your palette is actually a color reflection of your
sacred divine essence
So embracing it causes a dazzling presence!
Mother Nature is the greatest artist of them all,
And wants you to connect with yourself and fall
IN LOVE WITH YOU,
Can you hear the magnitude of this call?

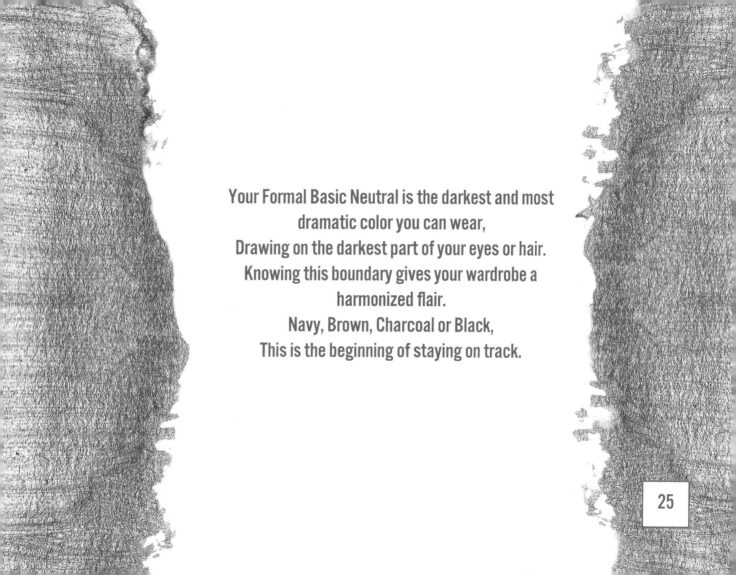

Your Formal Basic Neutral is the darkest and most
dramatic color you can wear,
Drawing on the darkest part of your eyes or hair.
Knowing this boundary gives your wardrobe a
harmonized flair.
Navy, Brown, Charcoal or Black,
This is the beginning of staying on track.

Basic Neutrals are the easiest and most versatile
of the group
Accumulating basics will allow your wardrobe to
loop,
As every color works with every color
The neutrals are often used as good filler.
Browns, navy, olives, burgundy and camel
I hope you are preparing to dazzle!

28

Your Eye Color is your color of Balance
When worn we align with our good conscience,
And evoke sincere rapport and trust
Wearing it when we want to feel close to others is
a must!
Your eye color is the mirror of your soul
And is great for feeling centered, for negotiating
and feeling whole.
It is the lightest and darkest part of your eyes
together blended
Others will feel so good with you,
be prepared to be befriended!

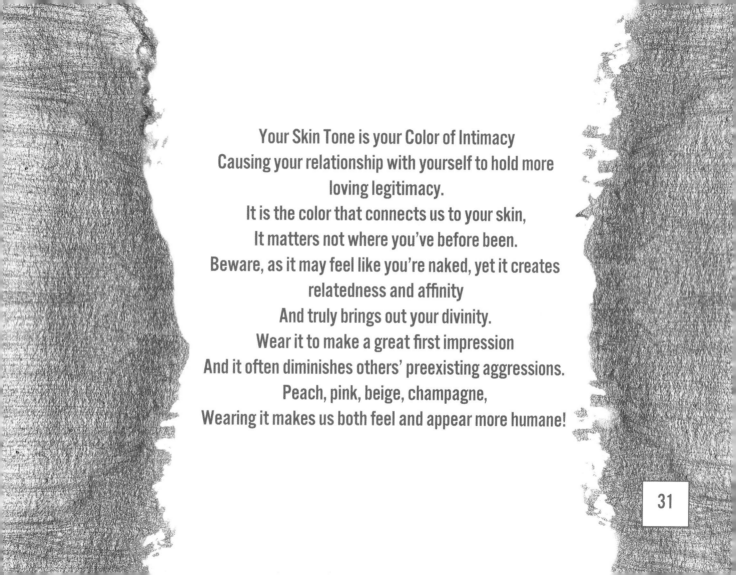

Your Skin Tone is your Color of Intimacy
Causing your relationship with yourself to hold more
loving legitimacy.
It is the color that connects us to your skin,
It matters not where you've before been.
Beware, as it may feel like you're naked, yet it creates
relatedness and affinity
And truly brings out your divinity.
Wear it to make a great first impression
And it often diminishes others' preexisting aggressions.
Peach, pink, beige, champagne,
Wearing it makes us both feel and appear more humane!

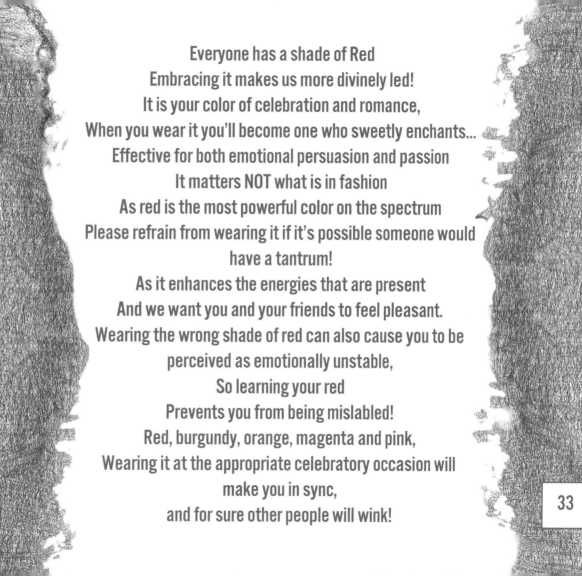

Everyone has a shade of Red
Embracing it makes us more divinely led!
It is your color of celebration and romance,
When you wear it you'll become one who sweetly enchants...
Effective for both emotional persuasion and passion
It matters NOT what is in fashion
As red is the most powerful color on the spectrum
Please refrain from wearing it if it's possible someone would
have a tantrum!
As it enhances the energies that are present
And we want you and your friends to feel pleasant.
Wearing the wrong shade of red can also cause you to be
perceived as emotionally unstable,
So learning your red
Prevents you from being mislabled!
Red, burgundy, orange, magenta and pink,
Wearing it at the appropriate celebratory occasion will
make you in sync,
and for sure other people will wink!

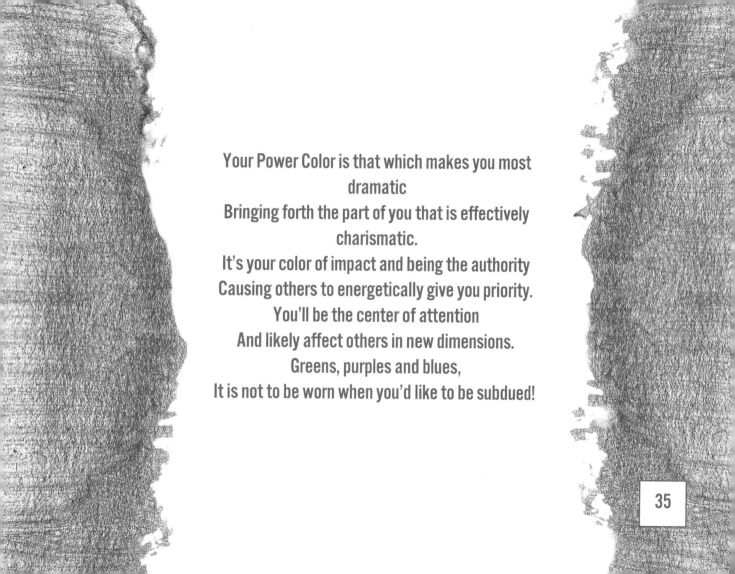

Your Power Color is that which makes you most dramatic
Bringing forth the part of you that is effectively charismatic.
It's your color of impact and being the authority
Causing others to energetically give you priority.
You'll be the center of attention
And likely affect others in new dimensions.
Greens, purples and blues,
It is not to be worn when you'd like to be subdued!

Your Support Color is for when you're working with other people
And desire to be low key
With intention to support and help others feel glee.
It's great for team building, passive relating and nurturing
And so good when you are in the role of counseling.
Violets, blues, browns and greens
The effect of the support color feels kind and clean.

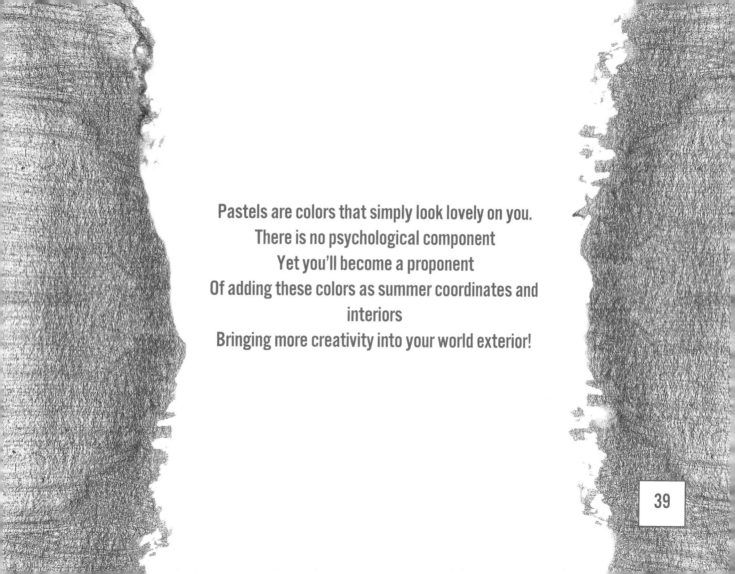

Pastels are colors that simply look lovely on you.
There is no psychological component
Yet you'll become a proponent
Of adding these colors as summer coordinates and interiors
Bringing more creativity into your world exterior!

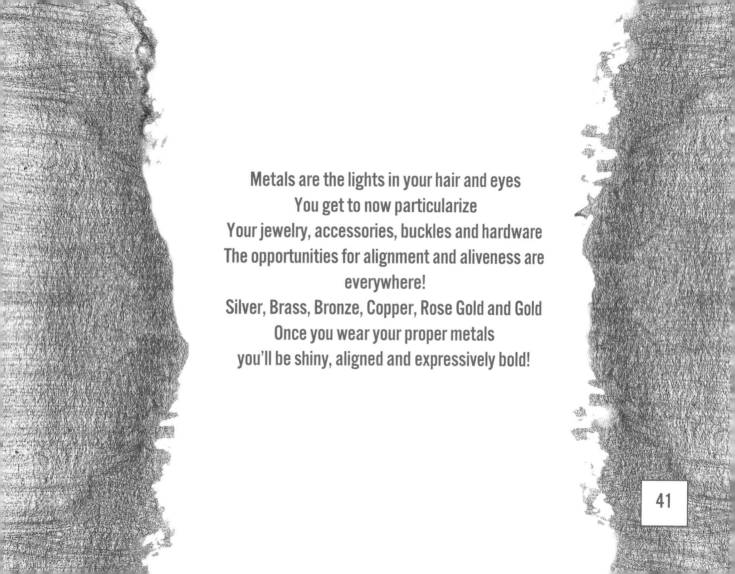

Metals are the lights in your hair and eyes
You get to now particularize
Your jewelry, accessories, buckles and hardware
The opportunities for alignment and aliveness are
everywhere!
Silver, Brass, Bronze, Copper, Rose Gold and Gold
Once you wear your proper metals
you'll be shiny, aligned and expressively bold!

To master this work takes time, patience and practice
Yet within a few years you'll be your own color expert emeritus!
You now get to be intentional in your dressing
Which causes your presence to become a world blessing!
As each color in your palette has a psychological implication
Practicing this work will create a wounding dissipation
And your friends, under curious observation,
Will indeed notice your powerful liberation!

44

Your Color Palette is the doorway into
The best version of you
and I am excited to see what you'll do!

Printed in Great Britain
by Amazon